Smart Pretender

poems by

Allison Joseph

Finishing Line Press
Georgetown, Kentucky

Smart Pretender

Copyright © 2019 by Allison Joseph
ISBN 978-1-63534-960-3 First Edition
All rights reserved under International and Pan-American Copyright Conventions. No part of this book may be reproduced in any manner whatsoever without written permission from the publisher, except in the case of brief quotations embodied in critical articles and reviews.

ACKNOWLEDGMENTS

"Newborn Cry Stirs Dying Mother From Coma, Family Says" appeared in the *Tusculum Review*.

The author wishes to thank the following individuals for their help on this book: Ian Moeckel, Sarah Schore, Kyle Stolcenberg, and Jon Tribble.

Publisher: Leah Maines

Editor: Christen Kincaid

Cover Art: www.cepolina.com

Author Photo: Rusty Bailey, University Photo Communications, Southern Illinois University Carbondale

Cover Design: Leah Huete

Printed in the USA on acid-free paper.
Order online: www.finishinglinepress.com
also available on amazon.com

Author inquiries and mail orders:
Finishing Line Press
P. O. Box 1626
Georgetown, Kentucky 40324
U. S. A.

Table of Contents

Instructions on Being Alone After Dark 1

Portrait in Yellow 3

Ghazal of the Withheld Kiss 5

Idle 6

Smart Pretender 7

Ode to the Artichoke 9

The Woman Who Lives in My House 10

To Emily Dickinson 11

Assault By Poetry 13

Nocturnal Ghazal 15

Mama's Cash Store Blues 16

Appetites 18

Parish Advice 19

Mom Fears High School Bullies Will Kill Her Daughter 21

Newborn Cry Stirs Dying Mother from Coma, Family Says 23

Meditation at the Ida B. Wells Birthplace,
    Holly Springs, Mississippi 24

Instructions on Being Alone After Dark

In the dark, you are no raven,
no crow with heavy plumage,
no power of flight when lights
turn on their haloes, buzz

of street lamps a tepid music,
sidewalks that in daytime
shone innocent and smooth
now rise up to grab your ankles,

trip your confident stride.
So you must step wisely,
carefully, saving the strut
for the sunshine, making

yourself small in the shadows,
light of your flashlight
guiding you past houses
that in evening obscurity

look like eager monsters—
doors unwelcoming, windows
afire with warmth you can't claim.
Hope that passing cars

hold no assassins, that
passing strangers pass you
without desire of injury,
that roadside ditches stay

uncomplicated, limbless.
Hope that barking dogs
stay chained, ghosts content
in ancient dusty attics.

It's never too late to reconsider:
guns, mace, self-defense classes,
the need to be a woman alone
walking somewhere the world

says she shouldn't, destinations
worth my time and days, my life.

Portrait in Yellow

Once I wore a yellow dress
that made a man want to love me,
that made me want to bare
my breasts to him, untouched
skin so ripe I shuddered
to view it myself. There's
something vulgar in the color's
confidence, the way it makes
flowers rude in their beds,
wet mouths of petal flash.
This color is childish—
hue of school buses
and rain boots, buttercups
and butter, bananas shedding
peels the way I wanted
to shed that dress, undo
the straps to let it fall
into a sunny pool at my
ankles, narrow stems
above my feet that I wanted
him to kiss and kiss until
I went molten, golden,
yellow behind my eyelids,
sun in my brazen hair,
all these little fires
starting where they never
were before. At twenty,
I didn't know any better,
thought yellow would make
him want me despite
other yellow dresses
on other hips, other lips
and tongues, other fingers
that might want him
unraveling their gowns.

If I could find that dress now,
I'd put it on this body
and love this body
more than any crush
of unexpected fingers
more than any pistil or stamen,
more than yellow tulips hot
in manicured beds, heavy
with fragrance, with ridiculous perfume.

Ghazal of the Withheld Kiss

I've waited quite a while for a kiss,
revealing every style for a kiss.

I slide my hands along a silken thigh,
I dream I trade her smile for a kiss.

Pout and rage, stomp through the house.
I'm acting like a child for a kiss.

My basket full of blushing fruits—
I'm wandering these aisles for a kiss.

Old-fashioned transistor on my shoulder—
I'm turning classic dials for a kiss.

No billy club, stun gun, or shut handcuffs;
Don't put my love on trial for a kiss.

I pace the world's long corridors.
I'm getting oh so riled for a kiss.

Before you leave, just let me announce
I'm caught in a state of denial for a kiss.

Idle

I think I'll stay in bed
and let the world slide by
no one has need of me
no one I want to guide

just let the world slide by
my limbs in lassitude
no one I want to guide
can spoil this attitude

my limbs in lassitude
my breathing deep and slow
don't spoil my attitude
the way I sink below

my breathing deep and slow
my sleepy yawning face
the way I sink below
means I've been touched by grace

my sleepy yawning face
my placid energy
means I've been touched by grace
a blissful lethargy

my placid energy
won't last beyond this day
this blissful lethargy
is seldom apt to stay

won't last beyond this day
no one has need of me
though seldom apt to stay
I think I'll stay in bed

Smart Pretender

I used to sleep with poets
I used to steal their rhymes
and trying not to blow it
I'd steal their finest lines

I'd steal their every image
their similes and style
whatever I could manage
I'd salvage for my pile

Before they'd rise I'd shuffle
through all their scribblings
stealing all their struggles
and all their ramblings

I'd pack my mind with everything
that they would write about
I'd imitate their rhythms
and push away the doubts

about my limitations
about my lack of skills
the art of imitation
supported me until

I found my independence
my small enchanted voice
no longer a dependent
I read them now by choice

I used to sleep with poets
but now they sleep with me
and though they might not show it
I'm in their legacy

I welcome every poet
who wants under my skin
what you'll find below it
is what you need within

Ode to the Artichoke

I come at you hungry,
anticipating the slide
of each emerald lobe against
my teeth, fingers slick
with butter melt and my
own juices, salivating
at all you hearty green
and bunched layers,
hairy and mysterious
in carnal longing.
I shouldn't wait so long
to have you, steam you
into submission so you
unfold for me like a
damsel, a buttercup,
flesh revealed until
revelation, nude irony
in my own kitchen.
How did I live before
I knew you, solid
round house on a stem,
in my palm, leathery
and intrepid, another beauty
to sink my teeth in, only
stopping when I scrape
each gleaming slice clean,
my hands and mouth glistening,
hot globe I have steamed then
submitted to, thistle gone
sacred—settled and eaten,
digested unto me.

The Woman Who Lives in My House

is a glutton, a slob, a cookie whore,
carbohydrate slut bent on licking

salt off every cracker, then putting
them back in the pack. Other me

is nasty—walking around naked to tease
the local dogs, dancing on flat feet

to no music but her own calloused
slap-slap on tile. Other me wakes up

and leaves you with the alarm on.
She breaks shot glasses, reading glasses,

glass figurines you've owned for decades.
She dines and dashes, won't do dishes

or laundry, but she'll eat every dessert
in your house, dropping layer after layer

of clothes she won't put where clothes
should be put—hampers or baskets or

or hellholes. That woman sneezes
on order, scatters germy wishes

everywhere. Fat chance she'll change
for you, for any of us. Devoid, deficient,

I can't tell if she cares that I wrote
all this about her, her naked body

so damn in love with itself,
you won't get an inch of mirror space.

To Emily Dickinson

Emily, my good woman, great spinster poet of those attic
    decades, persisting in your strange rhymes
    and hymnal rhythms—

I confess to you, your life was not as I
    wanted it to be, spectral vision
    of Amherst haunting all New England,
    plain-faced diva of the Divine.

All my teachers told me to admire you,
    but all I saw was that palled face
    gazing to nowhere, those clothes
    so stiff and burdensome that

I never wanted to be you, call you mother or sister,
    no desire to recite your spidery lines
    at school, not wanting death among my
    third grade dioramas—

I lived in the America of TV sets and roller skates,
    Flashdance and Barbie dolls,
    Jet Magazine and rainbow suspenders.

I was an instrument for everything but you:
    everything glowing and plastic,
    everything shimmering and glitter-faced,
    jelly shoes and Bazooka gum.

Lace collars and center-parted hair
    worked for you, but I needed
    a high-top fade, corduroy patches,
    Garbage Pail Kids.

Still, you did not stop for Death.

Still, you lived in a corner of my
        imagination, a willow I could pull out,
        a stranded tree, a locket with a
        sepia photograph, a feathered thing

I couldn't put away, bundled fascicles with
        their trellised words gathered
        like so many sachets, so many letters.

Who can deny you now, despite all your white
        fragility, unrequited loves, handwritten dashes?

I envy that attic in this noisy fatuous world.
I envy your quiet. Accept this tribute from me:
        common scribbler seeking solace,
        salvation, so different from you,
        so near to your wild nights.

Assault By Poetry

you're beautiful but vicious
you're gorgeous but you're mean
with all your moody switches
you don't make me serene

you're gorgeous but you're mean
you jangle all my nerves
you don't make me serene
with every heave and swerve

you jangle all my nerves
send blisters down my spine
with every heave and swerve
you swear that you're divine

send blisters down my spine
leave ashes on thighs
you claim that you're divine
permitting me to rise

leave ashes on my thighs
and bruise me 'til I'm done
permitting me to rise
forbidding me to run

you bruise me 'til I'm done
careen inside my skull
forbidding me to run
implying that I'm dull

careen inside my skull
attack my every cell
implying that I'm dull
and ignorant as well

attack my every cell
with all your moody switches
and ignorant as well
you're beautiful but vicious

Nocturnal Ghazal

Why must my love depart in the night?
It's bound to crush my heart in the night.

My mind delights me with its turns.
I'm feeling rather smart in the night.

I'm lying here, bored and aloof;
why won't you do your part in the night?

Shirt down there, skirt up here—
I'm dressing like a tart in the night.

You work my nerves; I nag your sleep,
our fights can always start in the night.

A jay can't fly if it can't drink!
Why can't I have a quart in the night?

Mama's Cash Store Blues

I lent you fifty dollars
you begged for fifty more
my wallet's growing smaller
you're buying out the store

You're sneaking out in darkness
behind your father's back
so immature and heartless
give me a heart attack

with all your plans and schemes
you're spending all day long
fulfilling all your dreams
while I'm left with a song

that will not pay our rent
or pay for light and heat
if I spent what you spent
I'd be a lot more sweet

more gracious and more witty,
financial diplomat.
But your debt isn't pretty
and I can't deal with that

Don't treat me like a cash store
don't send me all those bills
that make me spend my cash more
to solve your constant ills—

your screw-ups and your break-ups,
your drama and debris,
your tremors and your hiccups—
you need to live debt-free

So here's a bunch of want ads
(employment classifieds)
that money that you flaunted
just begs to be repaid

I've failed you as a mother
but now, I'm cracking down.
As long as you're my daughter,
this debt won't hang around.

Appetites

How can I live with appetites
that drive me hard with their demands?
I want to live, my body light
and free from all that contraband.

I try to follow diet plans,
attempt to savor every bite.
But late at night, hunger expands.
Why must I live with appetites

that won't relent, that make me fight
myself? I hate how my waistbands
indent me with their lines, so tight
they ride me hard with their demands.

I want to soar above the span
of turbulence, emotions slight,
not linked to food, its loud commands.
I want to run, my body light

and fast, all movement all delight.
Temptations lurk. Can I withstand
the constant treats within my sight,
live free from all that contraband?

I need to learn to understand
how much I need to live. My fight
is not with food but with the strand
of shame that makes me live contrite.
How can I live?

Parish Advice

Don't walk where you're not wanted
don't wear your dress too tight
you have it, but don't flaunt it
it's best to hide your light

don't wear your dress too tight
that style is not for you
it's best to hide your light
keep talents out of view

that style's not right for you
you shouldn't talk so loud
keep talents out of view
stay modest, not so proud

you shouldn't talk so loud
should learn to be discreet
stay modest, not so proud
life's better if you're sweet

Please learn to be discreet
keep quiet, neat, and meek,
life's better if you're sweet
we don't need you to speak

Keep quiet, neat, and meek
believe in what we say
we don't need you to speak
we just need you to pray

Believe in what we say
we elders know what's right
we just need you to pray
no backtalk and no fights

We elders know what's right
you have it; don't you flaunt it
No backtalk and no fights
Don't walk where you're not wanted

Mom Fears High School Bullies Will Kill Her Daughter
—WREG.COM, 9/16/15

It takes courage to raise a girl,
send her off to school, education she gets
a constant battle with other girls
who call her ugly, fat, and stupid

day in and day out, tripping her
in the hallways, making her crazy
with angry grief so that all she learns
is cruelty. I didn't raise a daughter

for her to be shamed day in day out,
because her clothes aren't right,
shoes not the right brand, body
too heavy for all their clubs and trips.

My daughter is smart, I tell you,
and beautiful, and when she came home
with her backpack ripped and face slit,
I marched right down to that school

to give those teachers and that principal
what for, came in there screaming
and yelling—and they told me to be quiet
or they'd call the cops and expel me

from the premises! I tell you who should
be expelled: these tacky little stuck-up bitches
who have been antagonizing my daughter
for weeks—hell, months now—those

snooty tramps who think they're God's gift
when they're really Satan's trash.
My daughter may not have boys
panting after her like sick dogs;

she may not have long fake hair
and open legs, but mark my words—
one day she's going to leave this
hell-hole greasy stain of a town

and she's going to make something
of herself—build buildings or fly jets,
or make advertisements like you see
on TV. Meanwhile these fugly bitches

will all be knocked-up, barefoot
and pregnant, no men left because
they've all left. My daughter will be
a millionaire. And she'll say

thank you, Mama, for screaming
your heart out that day—
letting me know I was worth
all the noise in the world.

Newborn Cry Stirs Dying Mother From Coma, Family Says
—*KSL.COM, 9/16/15*

Love is the longest sleep, the coma
that kept me from you until
I was ready to be a mother,
ready to wake and welcome you

with arms fit to hold, eyes
fit to see. You startled me
into my lungs again, plangent
cry tricking my heart into rousing,

thumping out of barest quietude
into full-throttle life. I don't
know what to call you: Lily
or Lucy, Regina or Alice,

little queen or soft soul,
diary of my thumbprint,
code of your father and me.
Little wit. Little darling.

Daring me to rise from this bed,
resist the monitor and feeding tube.
Angel made flesh, messenger
and passenger, your voice

will wake me so many more
times, shake me to my roots
when I'd rather slip back
into dreams that do not end.

You spurred me from that trance,
that spell, made me depart that
forsaken space, that gleam
of a starless planet, godless galaxy.

Meditation at the Ida B. Wells Birthplace, Holly Springs, Mississippi

This mansion built on the labor
of people dark as I am,
this white and spacious home,
fills me with ghosts

that are always with us,
our hanged and haunted
ancestors. This gracious Southern
home, made for receiving

guests, for the gentle brutality
we still won't admit,
stuns me this day, at this
turn off the highway.

Ida, you were a girlchild here,
stubborn courageous charm
in the midst of this mansion's
fireplace and banister,

this old Mississippi home
brought back to life
by the town's black hands.
The docent, that lovely

reverend, tells your history
in this house, her hands
pointing to pictures
and proclamations, says

her community fought to save
your evidence for future
generations, open to the public,
funded by donations.

Ida, I feel you here through
 refracted tears, explanatory
pamphlet in my grip.
 How can I ever be as fierce

as you were, unafraid
 when people—our people—
are caught by color in death,
 another one shot

everyday. How can I be like you,
 fearless in Mississippi,
in Memphis and Nashville,
 in New York and Chicago?

Wherever your words,
 your elegant fury
and hard struggle
 against injustice took

you, I will follow.
 I am your inelegant
heir. I will try not to weep,
 but to act.

Allison Joseph lives, writes, and teaches in Carbondale, Illinois, where she is Professor of English at Southern Illinois University. She serves as editor and poetry editor of *Crab Orchard Review*, moderator of the Creative Writers Opportunities List, and director of Writers in Common, a summer writers' workshop for adult and teen writers.

Born in London, England to parents of Caribbean heritage, she was raised in Toronto, Canada, and the Bronx, New York. A graduate of Kenyon College and the MFA Program at Indiana University Bloomington, she has received fellowships and awards from the Bread Loaf Writers Conference, the Sewanee Writers Conference, and the Illinois Arts Council.

Her books and chapbooks include *What Keeps Us Here* (Ampersand Press), *Soul Train* (Carnegie Mellon University Press), *In Every Seam* (University of Pittsburgh), *Worldly Pleasures* (Word Tech), *Imitation of Life* (Carnegie Mellon UP), *Voice: Poems* (Mayapple Press), *My Father's Kites* (Steel Toe Books), *Trace Particles* (Backbone Press), *Little Epiphanies* (NightBallet Press), *Mercurial* (Mayapple Press), *Multitudes* (Word Tech Communications), *The Purpose of Hands* (f Glass Lyre Press), *Mortal Rewards* (forthcoming) *Double Identity* (Singing Bone Press), *What Once You Loved* (Barefoot Muse Press), *Corporal Muse* (Sibling Rivalry Press), and *Confessions of a Barefaced Woman* (Red Hen Press). She is the literary partner and wife of Jon Tribble.

www.ingramcontent.com/pod-product-compliance
Lightning Source LLC
LaVergne TN
LVHW041520070426
835507LV00012B/1703